Your Guide to Government

How is a law passed?

Susan Bright-Moore

Crabtree Publishing Company

www.crabtreebooks.com

Crabtree Publishing Company
www.crabtreebooks.com

Author: Susan Bright-Moore
Coordinating editor: Chester Fisher
Series editor: Scholastic Ventures
Project manager: Kavita Lad (Q2AMEDIA)
Art direction: Dibakar Acharjee (Q2AMEDIA)
Design: Tarang Saggar (Q2AMEDIA)
Photo research: S Kripa (Q2AMEDIA)
Editor: Molly Aloian
Proofreader: Crystal Sikkens
Project coordinator: Robert Walker
Font management: Mike Golka
Prepress technician: Ken Wright
Production coordinator: Katherine Berti
Print coordinator: Katherine Berti

Photographs:
Cover: Ron Edmonds/Associated Press, J. Helgason/ Shutterstock (background); Title page: Rex Features; P4: Dennis MacDonald/Alamy; P5: Albo/Shutterstock; P6: Brian Seed/Alamy; P7: NearTheCoast.com/Alamy; P8: Iofoto/ Shutterstock; P9: North Wind Picture Archives/ Alamy; P10: Greg Henry/Shutterstock; P11: Chris Schmidt/Istockphoto; P12: Edward Todd/Istockphoto; P13: Misscanon/Dreamstime; P14: William Attard McCarthy/Shutterstock; P15: Mary Terriberry/ Shutterstock; P16: Visions of America, LLC/Alamy; P17: Rex Features; P18: Fritz Reiss/Associated Press; P19: Catnap/ Shutterstock; P20: Associated Press; P21: Stock Connection Distribution/Alamy; P22: Hans Punz/ Associated Press; P23: Thanassis Stavrakis/ Associated Press; P24: J. Scott Applewhite/ Associated Press; P25: Kenneth Lambert/ Associated Press; P26: Susan Walsh/Associated Press; P27 : Scott J. Ferrell/Contributor/Getty Images; P28: Greg Gibson/Associated Press; P29: Associated Press; P30: Pictorial Press Ltd/ Alamy; P31: Robert Wallis/Corbis.

Library and Archives Canada Cataloguing in Publication

Bright-Moore, Susan.
        How is a law passed? / Susan Bright-Moore.

(Your guide to government)
Includes index.
ISBN 978-0-7787-4326-2 (bound).--ISBN 978-0-7787-4331-6 (pbk.)

        1. Legislation--United States--Juvenile literature. 2. United States--Politics and government--Juvenile literature. I. Title. II. Series.

KF4945.B43 2008   j328.73'077   C2008-903637-9

Library of Congress Cataloging-in-Publication Data

Bright-Moore, Susan.
    How is a law passed? / Susan Bright-Moore.
        p. cm. -- (Your guide to government)
    Includes index.
    ISBN-13: 978-0-7787-4331-6 (pbk. : alk. paper)
    ISBN-10: 0-7787-4331-4 (pbk. : alk. paper)
    ISBN-13: 978-0-7787-4326-2 (reinforced library binding : alk. paper)
    ISBN-10: 0-7787-4326-8 (reinforced library binding : alk. paper)
    1. Legislation--United States--Juvenile literature. I. Title. II. Series.

KF4945.B75 2008
328.73'077--dc22

                                            2008025376

Crabtree Publishing Company

www.crabtreebooks.com   1-800-387-7650

Printed in the U.S.A./022012/UB20120127

Published in Canada
Crabtree Publishing
616 Welland Ave.
St. Catharines, ON
L2M 5V6

Published in the United States
Crabtree Publishing
PMB 59051
350 Fifth Avenue, 59th Floor
New York, New York 10118

Published in the United Kingdom
Crabtree Publishing
Maritime House
Basin Road North, Hove
BN41 1WR

Published in Australia
Crabtree Publishing
3 Charles Street
Coburg North
VIC, 3058

Contents

What is a Law?

Can you run in the halls at school? There are rules that say you cannot. Rules help keep people safe. Rules also make sure things are fair and things run smoothly.

We need rules when we are part of a larger community. This is why we have rules in school, at home, and even in sports.

Laws are special rules. A community makes rules to show everyone how to behave. Can you think of some laws in your community? Do they keep people safe? Do they make sure that everyone is treated fairly? Do they help make the community run smoothly?

Drivers must follow rules on traffic signs.

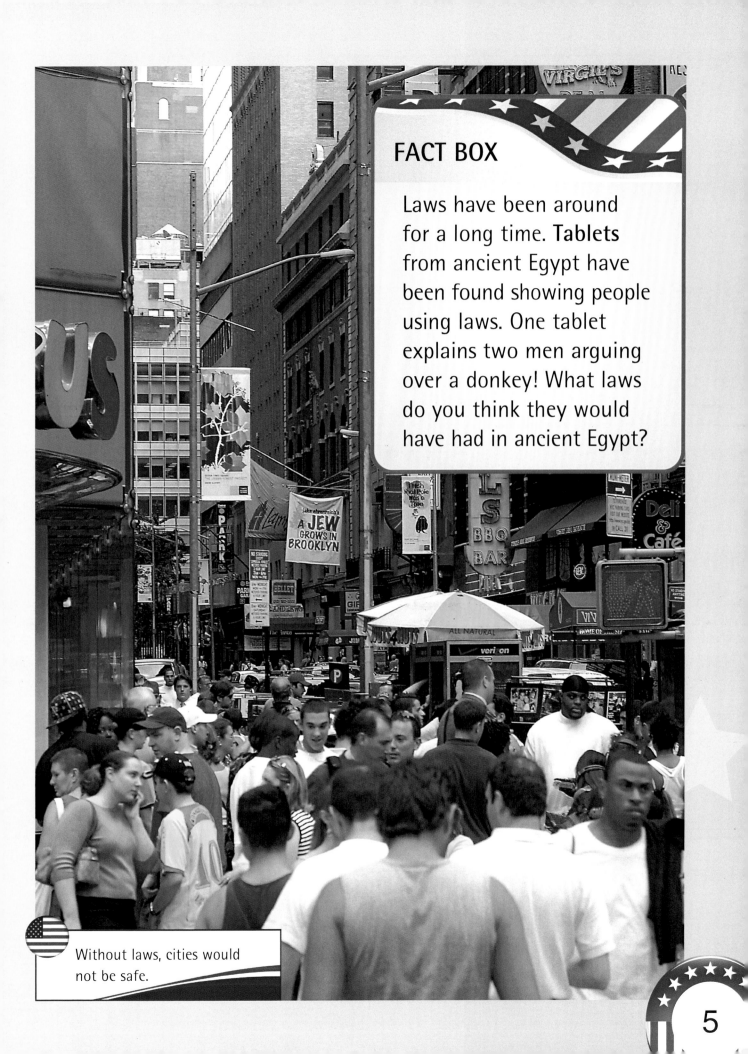

Without laws, cities would not be safe.

The Government

A **government** is a special group of people who make and enforce rules. In the United States, we have a **democracy** because we elect the people who are in our government.

We have many levels of government. Where do you live? You live in a city. The city is part of a state, which is in a country. Each of these places has a form of government.

A city council makes laws in your city. A state Congress makes laws in your state. Laws for the United States are made by the **United States Congress**. That is a lot of laws!

The people in this government meeting are making rules.

Governments decide what children should do while they are at school.

We need to follow all of these laws. For example, your local government decides what school supplies you need. Your state decides the subjects that schools should teach. The national government makes laws to ensure that every child can go to school.

Creating Laws

In the United States, we participate in our government by following the laws. We also participate in our government by helping to make laws.

One way we help to make laws is by electing leaders who believe in the same things we do. We can tell our leaders how we feel and what we would like them to do. We can write letters or send emails to our leaders about important issues.

Each family may have its own opinion about laws. This family may want laws that protect children and pets!

Laws long ago kept African Americans in slavery.

Back in the 1800's, teachers had to bring water to school, and boys and girls had to sit on separate sides of the room. Do these rules still make sense? Rules and laws sometimes need to change. New laws need to be created. Old laws may need to be removed or changed.

FACT BOX

In Mobile, Alabama, it is illegal to throw confetti. Why do you think this law was made? Should it be changed?

Is a New Law Good?

Imagine you notice school buses running while they are waiting for kids. You think it causes pollution and is bad for kids with breathing problems. You want the city council to make a law asking them to turn off the buses at school.

First, you need to discuss this law with many people. You need to show that other people are worried about pollution. You also need to talk to the city leaders.

Then, you need to show why a law is needed. You can have a scientist show how much pollution is caused by exhaust. You can have doctors show how air pollution hurts people. Now, you are ready to ask the leaders to vote on your idea.

Why is this rule good for everyone?

NO SWIMMING

These people are talking about a law they would like passed. Before an idea can become a law, people should talk about it.

People can suggest laws, but governments can, too. Government leaders may suggest laws to protect the people.

FACT BOX

Newspapers can tell people about problems and suggest laws, too.

Passing Local Laws

What if you wanted to make a law stating that local playgrounds must have fences around them? Would it be a national, state, or city law? Since the parks are in your city, this would be a city law.

Local governments are small. They can interact with people more closely. They may hold special meetings where people can voice their concerns or suggest changes to laws.

Since local governments are small, they are able to pass laws easier and quicker. There are not as many procedures to follow as the U.S. Congress.

Laws for this city may not be the same as laws for other cities.

Cities can pass laws to make parks safer, like placing sand under playgrounds to make falls less dangerous.

However, local governments focus on a smaller range of issues. They should make laws only for the local community. Building playgrounds is a local issue. However, there are parks such as Yosemite or the Rocky Mountain National Park that belong to the national government.

A Member of Congress

Our national government takes care of issues that involve all Americans. They are in charge of keeping the whole country safe.

Our United States Congress is in charge of making laws for our country. The Congress is divided into two parts called the **House of Representatives** and the **Senate**.

What kind of laws might Congress make? They make laws to ensure that people in the country are treated fairly. For example, they have laws to make sure wheelchairs can get into buildings.

This is a military jet. Congress can make laws that tell the military how many jets to build.

Congress meets here, in the U.S. Capitol.

Congress makes laws to ensure that people are safe, such as laws about airplane safety.

They also make laws to make sure things run smoothly. For example, they collect taxes to pay for the laws.

FACT BOX

Each state elects people to both houses of Congress. Do you know who your **representatives** are?

Congress Listens

Members of Congress represent their states.
They represent many people.

They must listen to the ideas of the people. They read letters and emails that the people send to them. They hold meetings to hear the people's feelings. They use these ideas to help them know how to vote on issues.

John Kerry represents many people as a member of Congress.

Representatives spend a lot of time reading mail, attending phone calls, and in meetings to find out what people want.

It is important for the representatives to listen to and please the people. If they do not, the people will not vote for them again.

Representatives must read many letters and emails, talk to many people, study the issues, and attend meetings. Each representative has staff members to help them with all of their tasks.

Making or changing laws is hard work. It is a long process. The staff members help the representative by finding out what the people in the state want. They also study the law so that the representative can make a good decision.

17

Lobbyists

Congresspeople are very busy. So, how do you get their attention? There are people whose job it is to get the attention of leaders in Congress. They are called **lobbyists**. A lobbyist's job is to inform congresspeople about an issue and get them to vote a certain way.

Imagine that you work in a factory that makes jeeps for the army. Congress is thinking about closing your plant and moving it to another place.

This means you and many other people in your city will lose their jobs. The workers could hire a lobbyist.

A rock star like Bono can lobby Congress to pass certain laws. So can you!

The lobbyist studies the issue. Then, the lobbyist meets with many representatives. The lobbyist then explains good reasons why the factory should be kept open.

Members of Congress listen to lobbyists because they know the lobbyists represent the interests of the people who hired them.

Lobbyists can try to change congresspeople's minds about closing factories like this one.

19

National Laws

Congress has three main jobs: to pass laws, to decide how to spend our country's money, and to make decisions about how we treat other countries. They are called the **legislative branch** of our government because a big part of their work is making laws.

Congress is divided into two houses: the Senate and the House of Representatives. Each house must talk about and vote on something before it can become a law.

Jim Bunning was a great baseball player. He then became a senator.

Look how many people work in Congress. It can be difficult to get this many people to agree.

How does an idea become a law? It starts out as a **bill**. A bill is a draft of a law. Bills can be introduced anytime Congress is present. While anyone can suggest a bill, it can only be introduced by a congressperson.

FACT BOX

Each state sends two representatives to the Senate. In the House of Representatives, larger states get more votes. California has 53 representatives, while Delaware only has one representative.

Studying a Bill

After being introduced, a bill is sent to a **committee**. There are many different committees such as education and transportation.

The committee talks about the bill. Can the country afford it? Does it make a difference for many people? Is it fair?

Committees have three choices. They can send the bill along as it is. They can change or improve the bill. They can stop the bill from going any further.

These members of Congress are a committee. Committees talk about bills and decide what to do with them.

Most bills "die" in committee. This means that the committee decides the bill is not worth looking at. Very few bills are sent along as they are. Most bills that are sent back to the floor are changed or improved.

Committees can talk to experts like billionaire Bill Gates.

A Long Journey

In the House of Representatives, the bill is debated.

In your class, you have rules about raising your hand before talking. The House has rules, too. People for the bill and against the bill are each given an amount of time to debate.

Once the bill has been read and debated, **amendments** or changes may be made to the bill. Any changes must be related to the bill. The bill is read and discussed three times before it is voted on.

Bills are discussed many times before a vote is taken.

Once a bill has been finalized, it is voted on.

In the Senate, the bill is read and debated. However, in the Senate, there is usually no limit to how long the bill is discussed by a member. Also, in the Senate, changes added to the bill do not have to be related to the bill.

FACT BOX

A member of Congress can suggest a new bill by placing it in a large wooden box located inside the Capitol Dome where they work. This box is called "the hopper."

How A Vote is Taken

After discussion, the congresspeople are ready to vote. There are different ways that a bill can be voted on in each house.

One way is with a **voice vote**. Members say "aye" if they are in favor of the bill and "nay" if they are against it.

A **standing vote** is similar. The speaker will ask everyone in favor of the bill to stand and be counted. Then everyone against the bill will stand and be counted.

This is a standing vote.

These buttons record the votes in Congress.

Another method is a **recorded vote**. People sometimes want to know how each person votes.

This can be done by **electronic voting**. Each person has an electronic card, which they use to enter and record their vote to the bill.

It can also be done with a **roll-call vote**. In a roll-call vote, each congressperson's name is called. Then, each person tells how he or she votes.

Why might people want to know how each representative voted?

The President

So far, the bill has had quite a trip. It was introduced. It was then studied by a committee. It may have been changed. It was then voted on and approved by both houses. So, is it a law yet?

No. First it needs to be signed by the president. The president carefully reads and thinks about the law. The president has several choices.

If the president signs the bill, then it becomes a law.

The president uses brand new pens to sign bills into law. Look at all the pens on the desk!

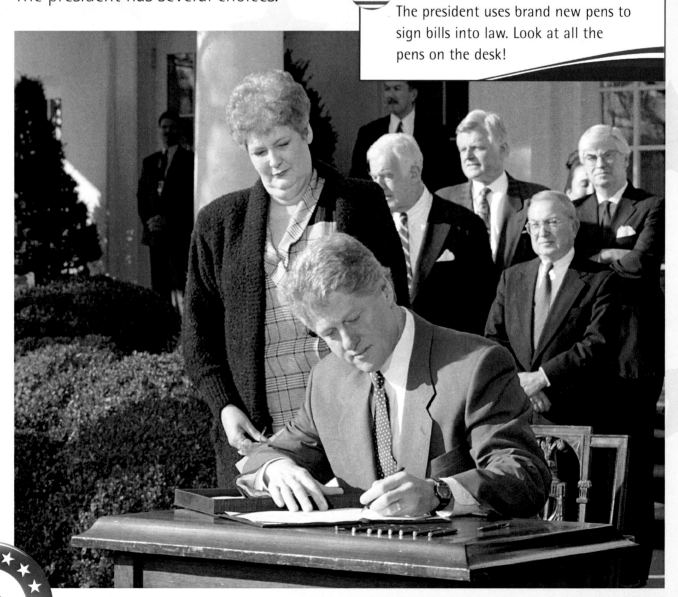

Presidents veto bills, but Congress can vote again to pass the law.

The president can also **veto** a bill, if he thinks it is unwise or not needed.

If the president vetoes the bill, is it dead? Maybe. However, it can also be sent back to Congress. The people in both houses can vote on the bill again. If ⅔ of the House of Representatives and ⅔ of the Senate vote for the bill, then it becomes a law.

Why So Much Work?

Local laws are approved much more quickly. Why is that? They do not have as many steps to be approved. Plus, less people look at the bill.

Why are there so many steps to make a bill a law? The laws that are made by Congress are very important. They affect every person in our country. Congress must look at them carefully and discuss them.

Imagine that a bill was introduced that made everyone use a recycling service. Recycling is good for our environment, but would this be fair to people who could not afford the recycling service?

So many laws are made, they fill books and books.

Working here could be dangerous. Congress makes laws to ensure work places are as safe as possible.

The laws made by Congress are very important to our country. They make laws about our military. They make sure our workplaces are safe. They need to make sure the bills are good before they become laws.

Glossary

amendments Changes to a bill

bill A draft of a law

committee A group of people who meet to discuss bills

democracy A type of government where the people elect their leaders

electronic vote Votes that are entered electronically

government A group of people who make and enforce rules

House of Representatives One of the two houses in the United States Congress

laws Rules made by a community

legislative branch The part of the government that makes laws

lobbyist A person who persuades members of Congress to vote a certain way

recorded vote Each representative's vote is written down

representatives People elected to represent you in Congress

roll-call vote Each congressperson tells how they vote

Senate One of the two houses in the United States Congress

standing vote People stand to show their vote

United States Congress The branch of the United States government that makes laws

tablet A stone or clay slab with carvings on it

veto Reject a bill or an act

voice vote People say "aye" or "nay"

Index

What are the levels of government?

What is a government?

How is a law passed?

How is a government elected?

CRABTREE
Publishing Company
www.crabtreebooks.com

ISBN 10: 0-7787-4331-4
ISBN 13: 978-0-7787-4331-6

50895

9 780778 743316